I CALL MY GRANDPARENTS "MOM AND DAD"

AUTHOR: Carilyn Rouyer

ILLUSTRATOR: Jonathan Hagar

DEDICATION

This book is dedicated to my grandson, Kayden and all the other grandchildren that are being raised by their grandparents.

Hi, my name is Kayden. I have the best mom and dad. I want to introduce you to my parents.

 My mom and dad look older than most moms and dads. That is because they are really my grandma and grandpa. But I call them mom and dad.

I'm not alone. Other kids are also raised by their grandparents. My grandma and grandpa explained to me that there are several reasons why moms and dads may not take care of their kids.

It could be their mom and dad may be in heaven.

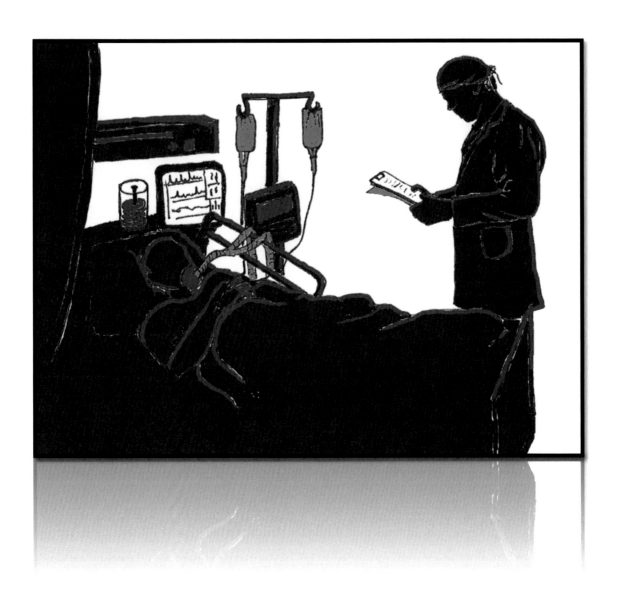

It could be their mom and dad may be very sick.

It could be their mom and dad made a bad choice and didn't follow the rules for being a good parent.

My grandparents explained to me that my mom and dad really do love me but are not raising me. They explained that they are being my parents and taking care of me.

They watch TV with me.

They rock me and tell me stories.

They feed me.

They take care of me when I'm sick.

They kiss me goodnight and put me to bed.

My parents are just like any other moms and dads except with laugh lines on their face and snow in their hair.

My mom and dad love me and we are a family.

Made in the USA
Columbia, SC
26 March 2019